Books by J.P. White

The Pomegranante Tree Speaks from the Dictator's Garden 1988
In Pursuit of Wings 1978

The Pomegranate Tree Speaks from the Dictator's Garden

The Pomegranate Tree Speaks from the Dictator's Garden

Poems by J. P. White

HOLY COW! PRESS
STEVENS POINT, WISCONSIN 1988

The author's thanks to editors of the following magazines where most of these poems or versions of poems first appeared: *Alaska Quarterly Review, The Agni Review, Another Chicago Magazine, Apalachee Quarterly, The Chowder Review, The Country Journal, Cream City Review, Cumberland Poetry Review, Hiram Poetry Review, The Indiana Review, The Massachusetts Review, Memphis State Review, Milkweed Chronicle, The Minnesota Review, The Montana Review, The North American Review, Northern Light* (Canada), *The Ontario Review, Pequod, Poetry, raccoon,* and *Tendril.*

The following poems appeared in *Poetry* (Chicago): "One Morning Another Good Man is Gone," "Vermont Gray, A Train, A Boat," "Why I Can't Live in Cheyenne, Anymore," "The Arctic Balloonists Talk to the Ones They Left Behind," "We Who Set Out for the New World," "In a Rowboat on a Lake in Minnesota," "Su Tung P'O Awakens in Moonlight to Write a Letter to His Wife," "Walking Pound's Canals," "On the Return of Halley's Comet," "Thanksgiving Night, Old Town, Portland, Oregon," "Walking to the Theater, I Tell You a Story about a Runaway," "To Confucius," "Playing for the Pickerel One August Night," "In Ecclesiastes I Read."

The poems "Invisible City" and "In Pursuit of Wings" originally appeared in *In Pursuit of Wings*, Panache Books, 1978.

The poem "You Will Write the Book" (from *Tendril*) appeared in the 1985 *Anthology of Magazine Verse & Yearbook of American Poetry*. The poem "On the Return of Halley's Comet" (from *Poetry*) appeared in the 1986/1987 *Anthology of Magazine Verse and Yearbook of American Poetry*.

The author is grateful to the Vermont Council on the Arts. Special thanks to Mac Miller, Bill Tremblay, Neil Shepard, and B. B., the poet docteur.

This project is supported by a grant from the National Endowment for the Arts in Washington, D.C., a Federal agency. Manufactured in the United States of America. All rights reserved. No part of this book may be reproduced in any form without permission from the publisher:

Holy Cow! Press, 5435 Old Highway 18, Stevens Point, Wisconsin 54481

Principal distributor:

The Talman Company, 150 Fifth Avenue, New York, New York 10011

For the Skipper and Betty White,
spinnakers, islands and the *Peregrine*

How, indeed, could art get along without the real and how could art be subservient to it? The artist chooses his subject as much as he is chosen by it. Art, in a sense, is a revolt against everything fleeting and unfinished in the world.
—Albert Camus

Contents

The Black Cat of Hilltop Provence

The Black Cat of Hilltop Provence

The coiffed poodles promenade past the boules courts
and later dine with their owners on bouillabaisse,
but the black cat of hilltop Provence
runs outside the radius of the dog's leash,
widening the sweep of its arc through lavender and mimosa,
up through the barbary fig and flowering agave,
out across the Roman viaduct to the medieval ramparts
where the air clears of traffic exhaust
and the olive and pomegranate seed make provision enough.

Thrown out of eternity
like a cinder spit from a volcano, the black cat of hilltop Provence
travels from cemetery to château
without ever leaving the red-tiled roofs angled into haze.
Sparks fly from its tongue, rough as quartz,
weathered memories curl asleep in its paws,
stories, knotted in its fur, tell of the great Germanic invasions,
the Moslem pirates, the sly cowled mercenaries
in love with the wired sex of history, the incendiary bomb.

Little sister to the panther,
brother to the stumbling defrocked priest,
there is no rendezvous with the morning's anonymous children
and the night's replenishing darkness it cannot keep.
Luck only will let you glimpse into its catholic eyes,
little Mediterraneans, drawing you into rooms of haloed martyrs,
swelling out, silver-gray to cobalt,
infinitely attentive or lazy or milky
with too much seeing from such tremulous heights.

If you find it on a perch, black as onyx baking in the sun,
ask it any question born of this enemy earth.

Ask the black cat of hilltop Provence
how to leap over giant earthenware jars, ochre-colored walls,
ask it how many vaults and arches you must pass through
before you reach the old nail-studded doors of the shepherd's church.
Ask the black cat of hilltop Provence
where to find the baby Jesus cradled against
the applied, calculated might of the vanquished desert zealots.

Go ahead, ask it what you will,
for nothing escapes the gaze of the black cat of hilltop Provence,
not the least of all grapes nestled in a bunch,
not the plump French women kneeling in sand and rubbing
their legs and breasts with perfumes and oil.
From where the black cat of hilltop Provence
sits on top of the sun, there is a place by the bluest of seas
for the nakedness of man and woman, the spilled religious blood,
the primordial smile holding ceremony while the icy pandemonium
            plays on.

Part 1

The Singer

The Singer

How should I be so lucky
   to wake with you
      high in the rafters

of a rickety house listening
   to a bird's bright string of notes
      lift June's sultry air?

Should we name this singer
   for everything
      in this first morning

we haven't yet heard
   and want to hear, oh so quickly
      and so slow?

This nimble plumage lit in your maple
   with a fiery trumpet,
      did you bring it round the Horn from China?

Or was it always near the edge?
   Can you answer my questions, sweetwater bird,
      nestled asleep in the high branches

between my neck and shoulders?
   Tell me your story
      broken from clouds.

My drinking roots
   have lived a long time
      to listen.

Touch the green in me
    with the rain of small feet.
        Dip, skim, cut the air I breathe.

Break sky. Ripple water. Pluck the earth.
    Do whatever you will do for your music.
        Nest the length of me with what you know.

Come back, now fast, now slow.

You Will Write the Book

Storms swirl off the Arctic Circle
Cutting the April of rural Vermont.
We have forgotten the calendar's promise
Of new life listening to the green.
The backyard nuthatch bangs his head on suet,
While you toss in sleep in another storm,
Thousands of miles from any recognizable flower.
7 months on 72-hour shifts,
You carried boys through slaughter.
Tongues, legs, scissors, endless syrettes of morphine
And the all-night fires clicking like locust.
What does this war ever give to you
But broken sleep and the voice of an orphan?
When will you not bring it back
To our table like ordinary bread?
That night in the anonymous airplane hangar,
Where they assembled bodies dragged from the delta,
You knew hundreds would be counted missing
If the proper pieces couldn't be found.
They would have nowhere to go,
But into another speech, by another president,
So you carried as many missing names as you could
Till you found enough white pages—
Their blank faces calling you 15 years later,
Out of this false spring, to write the story down.

The Nightingale Lights at My Window
and Tells Me How the Soldiers Had Their Fun

Being a nurse in Vietnam was a little bit like playing
sax for the dance band on the Titanic. The boys all
came over to have a good time at the war.
    —H.C.

Before we propped them up in boxes and sent them home,
all the boys wanted a sweet little
slant-eye in Da Nang
to doctor up the hole they drilled
into a thousand years of smiling.

Complicated,
this business of loving the war of legends—
winking its scintilla of lights like a barge queen
who owns every river on the meridian,
her crown studded with large stones, her panoply
suggesting both whip and rein,
bone ring and booty, and yes—
one glimpse of the eternal spume
connecting all crawly things to her upward gaze.

I read somewhere in the privy
history is a bear-pit waltz
tailored in the trousers between Eros and Thanatos—
a garden duet, as the great Dr. F. argued,
between fur and claw.
                    A lovely courtship for some
and a final unveiling for Missouri Bill,
who goes down with a dab of spittle to visit
the netherland of honeyed figs, Agent Orange
and the roaming chinch bug,

and learns quick
how to spin across the blank slate of beginnings
where the whispered coo squeezes the love button,
brings him closer to the long-awaited altar,
that commingling of souls,
the flickering union of kisses, blood and the ticket back home.

Christ, my blue-eyed boy, don't you get the picture?
With my needles, knives and morphine syrettes,
I played sax for the dance band on the Titanic.
Nothing like the pinnacle of a berg or a land mine
to bulge out a salute in a shy Christian fellow,
give him a hankering for the backside of a bullet.

You would take umbrage?

You, with your quivering umbrella,
your penchant for late night gin and backroads.
You would presume to never find your stripes
knee deep in the musk?
Even Christ was not entirely innocent
of picking up the scent.

I tell you the look in the eyes lingered
for any available entrance.
It was movie time. Bedtime. No time.
A good time to drop the mask and dog tag
for a romp through the land of planted thumbs.
Me. Them. Anybody. Who cares which hole?
As long as it's well-fed,
a stray dog will always scrap with a full-grown bear.

Believe me,
this feast of eyes bridges centuries.
It's contagious, even in a swelter,
like a sleigh ride on a patch of blue ice.
Look at it another way,
you who believe in the chortle of philosophers
and a teaspoon of reason before lights out:
in Nam, formlessness and true form
locked together at the neck and ankle
with nothing but air in between.
Think of it as a metaphysical gambrel, an heirloom of freedom,
and forget the "hubris" Herodotus brought home
on a broken tooth from the Peloponnesian War.
I memorized the divine clucking of a different gargoyle,
"Get your red hot, get your red hot tattoos . . . "
"Just you and me, Lord" wiggling up the length of a muscle.

On Sundays, I would hear from the morgue
(where I occasionally washed windows)
the soft invocations swelling in the throats
of the gum-cracking gunship pilots,
"Bless us, oh father of the seductive touch
and the swish of the glass-bead curtain,
for we have led the mechanical bird out of the nest
and dropped our fire on a scampering patch of heads."

While I dressed bandages, passed cigarettes
on 72-hour shifts, the boys would tell me
how beautiful it was, out there—a jubilee
like backyard Illinois peppered with fireflies
on a hot July night,
                          bodies careening through the light

of flares, the peek-a-boo luck of plucking
cross-hairs right smack on the clavicle,
the skin searing off like mist across the paddies.

Better than graveyard sex,
the chew of this jungle gristle.
Imagine the inside of your nails gone milky with steam,
that moment when you lift up the skin
of the earth's kumquat, peer into the folds
of sweating hair and swoon downwards, the body humming
like a three-day fever, blood jamming temples,
each moment a fresh nipple of Milk and Honey, each wish
flashing across your forehead telling you,
take it, my man, take it all,
and then, you know, "Bang bang you're dead."

Shall I blow a few more notes before the bow goes under?
Yes? No? At least pick up on this scat,
my sleepy-eyed poet, the one I keep overhearing
15 years without a church key or a church of my own.

Would someone spot me candy for this limp tool
    I need a boozy ramble in a foxhole
This inside straight makes me sweat
    Deal me another lick or cash me out with salt peter
Did you dick any gooks today
    Even a cow could sit on my face and get me stiff

Listen to me,
don't go to sleep, for the queen's barge approaches.

Your friend Pindar said, "Custom is king,"
so Darwin got a running start on a turtle.
I say who does not love the blur between dog and bear,
between enemy and friend, who,
tell me who in this century does not whittle his stick
into a club, who
will come forth without his splinters showing,
who at this late date and this far removed
from the last word at the world's tribunal?

Of a Night Fed with No Forgetfulness

The war never stops making holes.

15 years after Saigon and still you bolt awake.
I listen to leaves scrape against glass.
You hear in the throat of all that stirs
a blind animal noise. You wrap yourself up
in arms, cradling again a Tommy pitched
like a cinder out of a six helicopter collision.
You see orange light gushing black smoke.
Orders bellow to "forget what you can't save."
Legs gone, he lay crumpled in the hospital
hallway, a lump of coal, cast off to be tagged.
You stopped to sponge his eyes blistered shut.
His lips squeaked, "Somebody help me die."
You lifted the charred stump of him
into your arms and rocked to sleep his ashes
with needle after needle of nurse's morphine.
Your eyes sear into my shoulder, two bright holes.
"I'm scared," they say. "Nothing will go away."

In the Vermont Jungle

Why, what, when—it is the small link in the sentence,
the unfinished fugitive, that questions
who we are, continually appearing, disappearing—
the sound itself a wound gyrating in the mouth,
forcing us to live, or at least that was the story
she told one year when I stepped ashore a sailor,
and she, a Chinese nurse from a war America
had invented for the thrilling of the legal tender.
Through her, I cradled the medieval warning,
memento mori—a phrase thrown before the farewell
crusaders, and heard evidence of unscripted kindness,
impassable moments when one person must help
another die without knowing if love
is incommensurable with a creature of our level—
what some archeologists in the future may call,
a bottom-feeder of the sky. I tried to forgive
her anger in advance, but there was never enough time
to navigate a minefield without proper instruments,
and the intricate dishevelment of a similar history.
Only the nights in the bedroom were free to break
the chain of necropolises ringing the tiny village
where we lived above the Winooski River that snaked
every direction in and out of hardwoods.
In any jungle, there are reliable reports
of showers of milk, blood, luminous jelly and rosaries,
but no miracle fell from the sky that year
to uproot the past and make us new in the eyes
of the Unmoved Mover. We only cried out at night
with our apologies and our last minute annotations,
our fists beating down what brought us there
to that green world that conceals delirium and fatigue
and the knowledge that no matter how many tears
and seeds are spilled the war goes on written
in large letters that blur the small links of lovers' names
carved everywhere in oak and ash and maple.

Answering Your Last Letter

One season later,
And the ocean a black bible between us,
I remember your saying
We faced a religious problem
With our quiveringmost bones.
And I suppose, my Chinese orphan,
On more than one irretrievable night,
I did light a candle
In the chest of your weeping,
Wanting you to lead me checkered
Through a minefield
To the mangled home
Where you bandaged or amputated
Our young foolish patriots.
Belief or disbelief,
How can I describe my flight
Down stairs, over fences,
Out of car doors on the highway?
Everything can change
In the flash of a mortar,
And I never knew when your short-fuse
Memory would flare,
And we would re-enact the war,
Hacking each other apart,
Bound in some god-slave ritual
Of continual defeat.
Peace, when it came, merciful
And late at night, never restored
All the required articles of faith,
Still our bodies sailed out
On a flood tide in league with seabeasts
And sometimes the world's sorrow.

By morning, I never imagined
Our grip would stop your solo quest
Into the graveyard jungle,
Or that you would need to hover there
Forever like an orchid tearing
In the wind. Whoever you are
On that shore, with your well-thumbed maps
And one or two scars from Nam,
I know we are more in these letters
Than two lovers broken from the plum,
Something more than a casualty
Inscribed beneath the skin
Of this private era.
In a bulblit corner and frightened
Of recriminations coiled anonymous
In my palm, I see us both as part
Of the same imperfect shadow
That falls each hour
Over the torn Asian sea
And keeps on falling our whole lives
Until it takes us by the hand,
Asks us to leap into the chiaroscuro,
Forgiving the love we believed
Was ours to carry out to sea,
Across the longest war, and back.

The Dream of Swans in Moscow

The main hope lies in more and more individuals setting an
example of self-emancipation rather than longing for miracles.
—Boris Shragin, *The Challenge of the Spirit*

Angry father, sweet messiah, glass angel—

Even Tchaikovsky's swans fluttering at the street corner
Of your most invincible speech cannot wake you now.
Still, your hero's story climbs toward heaven.
As in March with cold cramped in boots and bark,
Slow moving lines of pilgrims, one day in Moscow,
Trudge from Alexander Garden to your tomb
To bless you with miracles, more lives.

Your spirit blazes on billboards, park benches,
In the Metro's electric web of tunnels:
You bent on one knee, sell children the pure cut stone
Of study. You spent on a plow, spoon courage
Into a peasant's mouth. From a Swiss street, in exile,
You feed critics a knuckling logic. You wander alone
In an ice wilderness, returning by train, triumphant

To Red Square. From my hotel overlooking your tomb,
I squint the rays of the Kremlin's red stars
Turning through wind. There, in starpoints
Balanced over boulevards, I shape the Bolshoi swans
In the night's vast sparkle. They weave across the stage
Of your dream like a white ribbon stolen by a breeze.
For 100 years, those slender birds have been swaying,

Feathering the scarred thumbs of your workers,
Holding again over midnight, the still arabesque.
Odette's pirouette cascades in a ripple of down.
Her neck folds into a wing, unfolds, twists
Downwards to brush the lapping waters. Balanced
At falling point, she reaches a new world
Through the lake's witching glass. In one kick,

Her wings molt to arms, breasts, legs, hair.
She leaps higher. Flightquills snap from shoulders.
Ice crystals swirl from wingfeathers. She glides
From the demon's spell into the arms of her Prince.
O Monarch of Paradise, white wings dazzle under glass.
And this fairy tale of swans is one you keep redreaming
Until it is perfect for your people and their dreams.

Near the theater of swans, neons flash, "Lenin lives again."
But what hope against hope does that light measure?
A new potato that rounds out the weathered vodka belly?
A first ticket to Bolshoi Ballet? A rose in the lapel?
You sold your platform well: children and tanks throw sparks
Into their prayers for you. Swans trumpet good over evil.
Red banners sprout in winter. Workers string colored lights

Across all bridges leading into this new city of the czar.
But what psalm will be sung tonight for this world
Of workers taught to forget the little gulags stranded
This side of paradise? From my window where I sit
And cannot sleep, red stars splinter night around my room.
Clock chimes from Spassky Tower lie in my head
Like large blank slate. I take the late hours to pray

That somewhere on the Steppes of Mother Russia,
One daughter about to dance rises out of the night pond
As the sky's great swan. Her eyes glowing behind the mask.
Her lucent neck unfurled for the long flight.
Her orange bill cracked with a low hiss,
Poised to strike against the black demon's spell,
And the princely rescue of your everlasting fairy tale.

Descending into the Moscow Metro

September, the sad vodka month in Moscow.
Rain, haze, rain sweep in layers over the city.
The sky, a dome of lead against which
No gold tooth glints with song. Each face,
The color of burlap, pulls against cheekbones
With the weight of traveling in the cramped hours
Before dark.
         "Reward comes only through suffering,"
Faces preach to me in the Metro's stained glass tunnel.
Christian law trudges them home the long way
Through tundra storm, barbed wire, blood.
Such a history of melting candles to endure—
20 million dead in this century alone
And no one talking about the State's many lions:
Their tireless, majestic jawbones grinding
Wax and ink into the creak of snow and slipping mercury.

Thanksgiving Night,
Old Town, Portland, Oregon

Look at this puffing city night
that never stops to count itself
broken into coins.
What grammatical construction
do you and I know by heart
that will visit the far-ranging human tones
chattering against the wind
of the Columbia Gorge?
Out on Couch Street,
the homeless can't wade through the snow
with their horse blankets
knotted around their throats.
One gent fishing for a pint
slides over ice with a jingle,
"Build you a snowman for 49 cents."
Everybody's in a jam
in this 3-season, slate-gray town
that helped invent the rain.
Even the one-day-only converts
crooning in the doorway
of the Union Gospel Mission
can't hang onto the minor notes
of Onward Christian Soldier.
On a night like this,
when we mumble from our pockets
and move along, what member
of our blood-kin can make
one or two gestures quotable with psalm?

Walking to the Theater,

I Tell You a Story about a Runaway

*Everyone has agony, the difference is I try to take my agony
home with me now and then and teach it to sing.*
    —Arthur Miller

That November, the gray-smelling cold gabbled
In the hot-air registers on 2nd Avenue,
Sent me reeling into the streets where white boys
Just didn't slide into the Apollo for soul.
I keyhole peeped, crept beneath stairs,
Craned my neck to spy on faces stranded
In flower-potted windows weathering
What little luck you could carry in a crime.
I prowled in the noise at every threshold
Unnamed in my native Ohio tongue like an angel
With an appointment to rehearse the doorway music
Scrambling the fish-net stocking legs of ladies
I wanted to meet. Anger, the old boomerang,
Hooked in my head, led me back over burnt lots
Where a house once lived-in leans into flames,
Sways beyond the reach of water jets and the cries
Of firemen who no longer crawl up their ladders.
I knew then that even the lucky ones who recall
Each 16-penny stud as it snaps in a wall,
Even they must go back each night over ground
Gained on the past to suffer the slap of fathers
Who never could explain the architecture
Of a burning house. My rendezvous down the neck
Of Harlem streets was a long honk and clatter ago,
Though just today I saw a cripple selling pens
In Grand Central who I swore was the same man
Who taught me how, at 15, to flicker my eyes

Into bulblight and panhandle with the best
Of the blind. What did I want then from my shadow?
A blond boy's lyric heaven bright with danger?
A knowledge sharper than love? To this day
I can only tell you about both sides of the whistler's
Street: how I wanted out and I wanted in,
To memorize the exact spot where this luminous city
With its many strange and unnerving gifts
Taught its agony to sing. For I knew if I was ever
Going home in winter I would need to pick notes
Out of platitudes, click my tongue into place,
And climb the unlit stairs to my room for more
Promising suggestions of what it meant to find a man
Curled around a fire hydrant, passed out, delirious
Or dead and know some part of me was him
With no bucket of week-old carnations to peddle,
And no family to button me up at the funeral.
I would have to dust off the ashes of the fallen
Pump organ and return it to my chest, wind it up,
Listen to it squeak or pound out a life I could rock to sleep,
And when it strayed too far alone, somehow, father and protect.

Invisible City

In the gutter
greasy men tug at my sleeve to sell me pulque and sweets.
Fat women in satin call to me from bicycles.
I walk through the streets, become lost,
stop and enjoy a woman's laughter,
run off after a wagon of melons.
How shall I live here?

Dogs circle one another
with their noses tied to dust in the road.
Two girls pace at my side, dream in my face of strong white fathers,
repeat my name to each other,
a password out of the city.

I dance with each of them in the fountains,
their wet black hair brushing my face.
I look into their eyes for a way out of my skin,
a bargain, but suddenly they are gone.
They exist and I do not.
Without them, I could no longer smuggle my elegies and jokes
into this space not filled with words,
this city suspended from cables
over a precipice.

How shall I live here,
where kites without strings fly all night,
where small fish swim in the marketplace,
where obese men, with red lips, hang over balconies,
where nymphs, dwarfs, bearded women and cripples
run the government in the streets?

The night sky slides over the city into an ice blue harbor.
There, ships are preparing to sail.
The white saguaro blooms forever in the lapels of skippers
who cannot sleep.
            I climb one of the longest streets
and watch faces float in with the tide, everywhere sprinkled
on the beach like cauliflower and snails.

How shall I live here,
where everyone I recognize tells me I look like a dead person
he has known, where each citizen

reminds me that the blueprint I seek
was burned with the city's father long ago.

In Pursuit of Wings

Father, I think of you tonight—
my body twitching in the dust from white liquor.
Your face is twisted, turned away from my perversions,
my drunken postcards from no address.
Every time I disappear into Mexico,
poems fly out of me like deadly birds.
That's why I'm here. I never wanted
to disappoint you with my basket of empty eggs.

Without a trade, yes, the streets are lovely with Madonna children
and there is nothing I can do but drift with the marketplace
in pursuit of wings. I never know where I will sleep,
in whose arms I will watch the sun climb out of the mountains.
Father, it doesn't matter what the poems cost. I must have them.

Your wings are called sails. The boats you've built from oak
to take the sea in the teeth with, are still rocking
under enormous white wings. I've loved those sails,
those hours standing watch all night, mesmerized
by the swinging of the compass needle.

But when I'm alone in this land, I see in the dust
my own lucent face, its many faces waiting for me in others,
why the sun is a falling child in every woman's doorway.
I stare into the eyes of a scorpion and know my death will be no
            different
from his, when the lava flows. All hearts, here, are stilettos
clicked into place, sparkling under an open sky.

Father, the roads do not end in winter. There is no ocean.
The sun is a black pearl I fish for in the eyes of whores
who smell the shape of death lying beside them and bathe the sinner

in a river of sweat. What else can they do, living this close
to the fire? One night, I will find it, that tiny globe,
and will tie it to the claw of one of my birds.

It will burn in your hands, my unreachable face,
a planet spinning without you, in need of your answering blue
current.

The Pomegranate Tree Speaks
from the Dictator's Garden

A few days after Somoza's assasination, the huge
tree in the palace garden sickened and died; meanwhile
people danced in the streets of Nicaragua.

On the forehead of a dancing people, drunk
With the death of Somoza, my leaves watch, unblinking,
A galaxy of blood. Each star,
A sparkle that divides by the nail.
Is tonight an open window, or an eyelid
Pulled back on the head of a bull?
My roots, planted from seed and tended
By a man shot to kingdom-come,
Have heard laughter chased before
In the alley like lucky dice.
But what ever changes in the animal belly?
The people who wired the commandante's car
Do not polish my fruit with their images:
Spider-web vendors. Pronoun hunters.
Us. Them. Somebody. Him.
Surrounded by a new string of flags,
My bark blackens with familiar readings
Of an anthem, implacable loves
Shining for all people. Then,
The tablecloth, the wine, the strummed guitar.
Tomorrow, the Chief will stumble over lines
Of his memorized poem.
                              Up here, the moon rays
Battle like transparent knives. Insects thrum
In my branches that have lived long with history's
Broken cart dragged over the orphan road.
For my part, my trunk prepares its own poem:

Mixed with dust and sadness, drawn from years
Alone in the garden, bearing witness to mules
Turning and turning round a ring for water.
What will my pomegranate poem say to the people?
How no one caught the scent of quince and magnolia,
Or brought one more chicken into the courtyard or saw
My candelabrum of scarlet gems torched by the sun.

Part II

Apple Blossom, Oriole, Lilac

Apple Blossom, Oriole, Lilac

for David Mura

The empire in confusion. Loss of memory.
A polished agenda broken from its laws.
Still, May returns with a readiness for creation,
the stars arranged by zodiac as if in final greeting
and farewell, the living stuff of both
having skittered from the egg. Now, the modest
ornaments of our garden dangle into view—
apple blossom, oriole, lilac. A jubilation
for these agile gifts speeds across the sleeper's face
nestled in peppergrass—there, in the palm, suddenly,
proof of Paradise, the flower Coleridge presented
as a pledge of having braved the severed upper realm
and returned. All this blossom-knowing
with god in exile, roving like us up the manifold
tableau of the universe. Only how could it be
to contain at once the Five-Petaled Mist
of the Apple Blossom and The Gathering of the Sparks,
each of us a fire, as Heraclitus said,
mixed with spices and named according to a scent
caught in smoke? Here, in my country,
there is little heart found in the upright,
Heaven-facing fathers, while, overhead
the oriole suspends a pendulous nest
on the swaying outer branches of the cottonwood,
and abroad, one more lyrical revolution
in love with fraternity, devours its own children,
forgets the purple lilac found in the moist clay
of the village church. This season
no country on the tilted axis will accept,
as proof of Paradise, the poverty of our ideas—
apple blossom, oriole, lilac. Only the animals
waltzed through storybooks may come to drink
of these scents, come at last in pairs
when the night holds sway over the bowed head,
and the garden is free of strangers.

We Who Set Out for the New World

I would like to tell the queen
How we suffered in our search
For the golden palaces of Cathay.
I would like to say the north wind
Broke our knees, maddened the compass,
Our ships two years spun off course,
Our mouths cracked by tar and rope.
After all, we had voyaged
Off the salt's edge, holding breath
As we entered sun, dumb faith
Fished from our shields
When Rodrigo de Triana nimbled
The crow's nest, followed
The wings of a Man-O-War
Back to the miracle of a globe
I carried in my head like music.
Tierra. Tierra.
His cry planted the seed
So the ancient conquest could begin
Again. But how could I tell her
What gold we found, glittered like sand?
What jewels flashed beneath our bowsprit,
Filled our baskets with a thousand
Rainbow-scaled fish?
Under moonlight, we lay charmed
By the iguana's fragile night whistle,
The switching of its tail in sand.
Bougainvillaea, lemon, hibiscus—
The wind stung sweet, slow,
Always ripe with rain.
This New World, patched in blue,
From baby's breath to ink,

Lapped against the hull of the body
Like the first cradle song,
Taught us how to question
Her unraveling reproaches
Thrown like pebbles against the shore.
After we anchored peace with the natives,
Honey-skinned, naked, swaying—
What did her flag mean
When we played for hours
Among the greens and yellows,
As if for the only time,
Without force, without power?

1984

Children. We had grown into children
Of a lesser order, unquestioning,
Distracted, easily amused—each alone
Like a flower that every morning
Slowly opens its eyes, gazes
Without reproach at the gardener
Who cuts and bleeds the stem.
On the legendary isle of happiness,
No written word caught in the craw,
Essential as bread. Many just drank,
Or looked on as angels, forgetting
To raise voice when the roweled heel
Of the general spun over the dead.
Others shopped all hours for bargains.
We heard in the click of engaged gears,
A truth sent down by the authorities.
We could not conceive of fire,
Hunger or the sword, that the date
Of our execution had been fixed
By an old thin man with shiny boots
And a riding crop. Call this life
In the flowerbed, a failure
Of the imagination, call it fear
Of the soil eroding, the sky falling.
But this much is certain of our childhood:
If Hell guarantees its young
Magnificent quarters, silk robes,
The sweetest cakes, all possible pleasures,
Yet condemns them to live
In ignorance, nodding among sticks
And stones as one more fallen stem,
This would be punishment enough,
This would surely disappoint the gods
Who we said would hold our last days from harm.

The I and the Not I, and the Ancient Rudder

Creature or creator, who is to answer
for our spiced indulgences of chanterelle
and avocado on this summer evening
beneath the soft flapping of sailcloth,
our bodies leaning over water with a light shine?
What a history swirls inside a single "I"—
the multitudes of people laughing, shoving,
all lusty for what pulls away from shore,
what swings close. For our portion under shadow
of the eagle's claw, we too hanker after wind
and new orders—for what other violent contest
could we claim for the Republic? Here,
democratic coin sweats in sewn leather.
Crowns on lofty heads wobble like dice.
Gossamer itself will have to swing like Brooklyn cable
before the States mark the soul's progress.
The self-made and the self-evolved
stand opposed with not even a gimballed language
between them to cancel tyrants and father gods,
and even Whitman, that good gray wound dresser
of the Civil War, slept with a dead bolt
thrown against the scattered etceteras
prowling at dawn. Push out the foolish boom.
Who we are downwind on Lake Calhoun flies till dark.
There is no telling how freedom's experiment
will end—or whether you and I in our jury rig
will find direction in a series of unlikely jibes,
or whether the blind carp we saw below the dock,
or tomorrow's bloodline will be the carrier
of higher goals, or whether the breeze—
wished for and willed—can hold our many divisions,
born of plunder and hope, against
the ancient, angled sweep of the rudder.

On the Return of Halley's Comet

Omen, apparition, long-awaited peacock's tail—

who will not ask you, as you flicker fifty moons wide,
of news from some other earth, afraid for this one?
Is there another world for us to embrace? More lives?
Or do we shuttle like you, back and forth,
from black to blackness, an unaccountable freak,
an orphan among stars? In our written history,
we cannot keep the appointment with the Self—
the hour when the fist breaks, opposites crystallize—
while you double back out of the ox-blood arctic
of Jupiter's gravity, across the Babylonian tablets
and the lives of Confucius, Attila the Hun,
Seneca, Cortez, and Twain—a matchflame lit
from ice hurtling through necessary violence.

Your eternity remains a predictable seduction
with each of us here plunked into ground,
a branch of star wormwood tangled up with the beyond.
Three million years ago we did not share the slumber
of the tapeworm's eyeless world. The last three
thousand were given to clashed swords, ghostly sparks
and ornaments, and perhaps, only the next three million
will tell if the earth will take cuttings watered
with sweat in years of drought, if our poor roots
will cut to the fat loam, draw blood from eternity,
make our moment mortal and understood, or whether,
like you, the crown of the skull will remain as wide
as the heavens above and as difficult to read . . .

In Ecclesiastes I Read

In Ecclesiastes I read,
"That which is far off and exceeding deep,
Who can find it out?"
Who can tell the earth's tale of wearing down,
building up, erosion, creation,
a swirl of embers breathing amethyst and tourmaline,
a suffering bounded by the four baleful rivers of Hell
and a sun that will one day collapse,
engulfing it in one long dragon breath of dying out?
The ancients said earth was immovable—
that every daffodil and sequoia
was fixed in its own sky-blue mirror.
Now we know this planet is like others,
restless, driven, continually torn apart
and reassembled by a shifting of plates
grinding beneath the surface like nervous molars.
The globe itself a work in progress
with its iced poles wandering
and its fires bubbling below the seas.
Even its path through space
is an egg-shaped, elliptical orbit, hardly circular.
It is here on what used to be called solid ground
that we live—fragile, torn by our need
for love, food and mercy.
Most of us worried there will be too little time
to light the lamps of our fingers
and walk the narrow path in the rain.
But what of the earth? Who can find it out—
embrace its drifting continents,
who can love it as it is—unfinished,
smudged with the dust of rare constellations,
flickering on and off like a rain-drenched fire in the woods?

In the St. Paul Science Museum

For death there can work no algorithm
that will bring the upward-tending burning breath
back to the little hours knelt beneath sky.
Natural law counts no numbers or names among the fallen:
the parliament of carpenter ants will hold court as always,
pronounce the newly deceased as fair game
for shoring up the nest.
Though the family dog bends its howl into thin strips of rain,
the fool's parsley and feldspar will glitter
on the grassy slope overlooking the homestead.
The sleepy lizard will curl between the bricks
where the mortar has crumbled, and everywhere blue-eyed children
who will have wandered upon the glass viewing cases
will mistake the pointing finger for the crescent moon.

In the St. Paul Museum, for example, generations milled
around the mummified Egyptian priest, the caved-in cage
of his body blackened beneath the half-opened shroud,
his toenails still aglow with dabs of honeyed oil.
What wonderment suspended over the body!
Such high-pitched shouts of glee! To think
this man once calculated the distance between serried stars,
danced across oceans with monkeys and elephants,
balanced the heavenly empire on the eye of an obelisk.

Winter Milk

Up there, through the serpentine snow
winding down from nighteye blackness,
the Horsehead Nebula soars in Orion,
just within reach. Aside
from a few close neighbors, all other galaxies
are pushing away at the speed of light,
going, almost gone before we can tilt our heads
to catch a few flakes on the tongue.
Winter milk, we used to call it—
what you could tongue-lap from the unseen.
Reason, then and now, too feeble a god
to worship on a blowzy night like this
ferreting the life-sustaining snow falling
between stars. Conrad was right.
We are camped in a garish, unrestful hotel—
bewildered travelers with darkness awaiting
at either end of the line. We arrived
in winter with contrary instructions:
do we reel under the weight, or act swift,
feast or fast, lay still like the jungle wasp
who makes of her tarantula a willing victim,
or, out of necessity, grow a new thumb
from wristbone? What inventiveness
can we enter into the gaze of the far-away
white horse? Only the questions raised
between stars are indestructible tonight.
All else must contemplate its molecules
rearranged. Even the flea buried
beneath the rotten apple must become
a philosopher and analyze the cost of progress.
Back home, a child asks in crayon,
if we will be the first to feed our people

into the figuring machine. And here,
we walk between essays, constellations,
ancient calendars, traverse familiar streets
with a tongue that feeds and feeds,
not knowing why or from whom this milk suddenly comes.

Christmas Eve Without Starlight

In December, most nights never break loose from clouds.
Whatever star cluster there is
Swirls out of sight.
Tonight, the wind writes the old alphabet on snow
And we can now report
The pall of permanent winter—
Clouds leaning over the earth
Like a shade pulled down
In front of a candlelit window,
Until, from cap to polar cap,
Our bright, spinning planet
Slips completely from view.
We cannot see out and we cannot be seen.
All the light we have
Is what we have in us,
Just the smallest beginning point of light
Rising out of marrow
For a glimpse of the coming nativity—
Not out there jeweled above
The shepherd's winter trek,
But here in me,
In my own lowly barn,
Where I rake the last of tonight's steaming cow dung
Into the trough, pitch fresh straw into stalls.
In me! Imagine the audacity!
To sit until morning among the animals,
Rocking myself as one new infant,
A gemstone shining without stars,
The loveliest of lights
On this ridge of Vermont granite,
One looking for many.

The Hour the Ships Came In

Only through a pearly shimmer could they be seen at first,
the hour the ships came sailing in from all nations.
Through scattered clouds, the color of apricot fish scales,
they all heeled like high wandering birds
outdistancing true north and the lessons of weather.
You could see them—the unbreakable tall spars,
the barnacled steel hulks, the tar-smeared diesel tugs,
the sleek pleasure yachts. They all came together
in one phosphorescent hour sprung from the block
of petrified time.
                            There was no telling the how or why
of it—when they all swung toward shore across the sea
of reptile hours washing over good and evil alike.
There was no telling if from the separate distances
of their salt lanes they had finally glimpsed
the passing shadow of flesh pulling for spirit,
or if a seasick bumblebee or goldfinch lost
from the seasonal migration was now braced at the helm—
the impossible benevolent captains commanding a flotilla.

There was no telling the truth of such a difficult passage
or who had buffeted the ice-jammed routes or suffered
the heat spasms of the horse latitudes in the south.
For those on board—in all their chattering tongues
swollen with god and politics—what had they known
of the sudden compass swing, in that moment
after the passing of lanterns and the misery of bells
caged in the fog, in that second of the somersault
when fear and prayer fought for sentinel in the spine?

For those people, queasy and invested in their own inscribed
scars, was all of history forgiven in that hour

or simply brought forward as one memory of the earth's
dizzy trial by fire? Between the easy syllable sway
earned by the conquistadores' whip and the clenched
landowner's jaw polished in the jungle paradise,
there were no answers shouted from the crow's nest,
only this hour when you could imagine the crossing
of incandescent eagles—even though the past, dragging
its seaweed memories, could not have been far behind.

Out of the unpredictable, snaggletooth sea,
past death, cool as a lemon's breath, past doubt,
loud as the chafed rope in the masthead pulley,
past even the future, smooth as the belly of a blackfin tuna,
they all came in—the flagship fleet, the mint-lustre
gold bar fleet, the pomegranate and oil fleet,
and the imperial gemstone lion's head gunship fleet.
Like the whisper of solitary criminals repeating
a scratched message through a wall, all the hulls rose
and fell and pushed forward through their own echo.

And no matter how rich the cargo below decks, no matter
what price it would bring in the distant, foreign markets,
they all came in—not to plunder or lay siege,
not to preach from the throat of a gilded figurehead,
not to show off the sweet spider bite of the slave girl.
With no forced Hosannas, no serpent hisses,
no barging for the most favorable anchorages,
they just came in, and for this one hour,
the remote became the near-at-hand,
the argonauts of the unseen rode in the harbor

and watched the colonels and the shopkeepers
who had taken up a bird's-eye view and a sharp pencil.
All the ships from all the nations came in,
even though the risk of giving too much,
or not enough, by the time they arrived
was too great. Even though there was no hope
of them all catching the next sailing tide.
Even though the light was failing in the early morning
and all the hours in the world
had already passed from their delicate tinkling brass clocks.

Part III

Cutthroat on a Full Moon

Cutthroat on a Full Moon

I climb one creek for three nights
to find the snow-banked lake of Ute legend
where the cutthroat took its name from the moon:

the tribe's oldest trout slept all winter, a fat thief
belly-deep in mud. When light struck his glazed eye,
he rose toward its beam with an unhinged jaw.

He leapt so high, he gashed his throat
on a piece of jagged moon and fell back to earth
with a sash of red draped across his throat.

A song to cutthroat clicks in my blood rhythm:
"Cutthroat snap a full moon on a dry fly,
he's a bright light, getting brighter, till he dies."

I flick the tune to the arc of my fly rod
and wait for the moon's light to steal
upon us both at the creek's source.

My body roots in snow for the jolt of him
shooting upward through light split bamboo.
Out there, somewhere. Coming up.

Slowing finning, dappling the surface,
cutthroat turns and breaks cover to feed
on the image of himself dimpling the moon

with the swish of his tail. I cast out
to the water's shine, hook him through the moon
rolling beneath the lake like a bruised and smiling face.

The finger tug of my line thrashes down to bottom,
holding me quick to the small life
I will give back when I go.

Halloween at Shoshone Geyser Basin

for John King

We straggle north off the Pitchstone Plateau,
two souls caught in summer gear by first snow.
Everything hurts down to bone
except the dream of the earth's old bellows.
Two miles more: smoke puffing through iced aspens.
We sight the first geysers, run to sample
with our eyes each bubbling pool of water:

pot boilers, smoke jumpers, whale spouts,
cauldrons, moon cones, steam vents,
mud pots, fumaroles. All are phantoms of fire.
We hear a geyser's half-minute tones
like bees churning a knothole in the ground.
Is this the same watery hiss the Shoshone heard?
Is that why they left their huts one night

and vanished to the south in October
as the snow whistled in to roost?
John and I circle the basin, hobbling on frozen boots,
swearing at the earth's lava to ignite
our snow-struck bodies dreaming of a hot river.
He sparks fire from the underside of dead pine,
stripping bark before new snow wets the grain.

One dry twig snaps. He fans a crackling branch.
I hover over a crater's scalloped edge,
welcoming heat into my locked limbs:
chartreuse pool simmers delicate bath water
terra cotta glitters with suspended silica,
turquoise jets pure nova, the one mesmerizing me
like a swimming pool on a dog day in Ohio,

teaching me now to lean forward, sing through the cold:
"I have a body, but I am not my body, I am more than this.
I have a mind, but I'm not my mind, I am still more."
My eyes close until my spirit returns
to sing the voice of snow. I drift up
through the water's revolving prism changing color
as I near the bank. Dead Shoshone awaken

in the steam bowls and sulfur terraces of my singing.
They gather round me in their masks,
blessing my body's rainbow refraction, my sinking into fire,
my ashes in the water, my voice letting go of the cold,
settling into steam, now quiet, now singing, now quiet,
because in the spirit of this valley there is no room for death,
only for testing, for pushing on.

Bushwhacking Through Bear Country

Knowing he is here,
The wind flares in our nostrils,
Bringing pinesap, larkspur, paintbrush,
The old smells, one at a time.
Civilization falls from our shoulders,
Becomes once again spacious,
Jagged, alone—with fields, with trees.
The days turn to face his roaming miles
Up in the deserted meadows
Along the banks of the Firehole River.
We imagine him
As every gnarled trunk,
Split with lightning,
Hunched, root-grubbing,
Bigger than any mountain
Rumbling with magma.
Our fear keeps him lumbering
Through huckleberry bushes,
Swiping the last September jewels
To frost the tips of his winter coat.
Once, fording a creek at dawn,
Shoes slung about our necks,
We let fear drain through our feet
Into powdery blue stones,
And he stopped to watch us, curious,
His eyes squinted into sun.
Finding his print on the other bank
Gave us answers:
Dark, deep enough
To swallow a whole hand.
When we placed our palms on moist mud,
A shiver shot up our arms,

Filled with bear-strength.
We stood up, gulped
The crushing air,
And knew he swung near.
Off across fields of buffalo grass,
Tall enough to hide him on the run,
The Tetons broke clear from the first flurry.
The sun opened the canyon with amber light.
The morning stood bright in any direction
With the scent of him stung in the air.
This was a place
Our bodies would remember.

Why I Can't Live in Cheyenne, Anymore

Because the gray pebble wind never stops.
Had you been there, when my house flexed
On its studs, I might have slept, not heard
Coal trains switching rails, thundering East.
I might have dreamt through a truck convoy
Punching gears for the last wedge of pecan pie
At Little America, a diesel pump home, home
On the range. We could have joked about dogs
Roaming in packs. Alone, I spooked into a curl,
Banking on sun to nip their howl. "Believe me
And come back," I wrote. "Nights on the plains
Never end." Take stranded Monday. I belted
Gin with this cowboy spangled in spurs. 100 years
Too late to ride fence, he'd driven hard
From Chugwater or bonecold Gillette, 150 miles
To yip at a Bo Derek flick. En route, he catches
His cowgirl, perfect, flagging his wheels:
Hair streaming blonde, dangling fruity lips,
A woman, half-child, born of the sagebrush
Tabletop, fed on the milk of its hailstones
And the rockabye of its runaway boxcars.
He swerves to her shoulder, flings open the door.
"She blew me a kiss and was gone," he tells me
At 2 a.m. in the O.K. Corral Saloon.
The wind's whipping post, Cheyenne. No woman,
Real or imaginary, could love so much punishing
Horizon. But how about a visit? We could bowl
For beers, croon with the pack for a twister,
Hit the Union Pacific depot with no luggage
For one-way tickets out of the wind, anywhere.

Night Ski in Vermont

Blacked in branch shadow,
I am the owl's swiveling head,
the rabbit's crackling fur,

the buried grouse about to drum.
With my eyes shut, I hear
each branch and needle walking

towards me for my touch.
I dip my tongue into the origins
of this element broken

from a dark and riddling storm.
A brook breathing beneath
my kick and glide tells me

I can sing with the solitary birch
about new bark for the spring thaw.
When my head stops fueling the struggle

between the uphill and the down,
my skis kiss the snow
with a song-dog stride.

Tonight, I am one singular motion
connecting the forward edge of shadow
to the bright bed of sleeping snow.

Here, I drop my life's questions,
and slip out beyond the brain chatter world.
I climb the face of a wind-bent ridge

and listen to the cold working through me:
in a place sculptured and still
where the gods we sometimes cry out to

lie in wait for our tracks to reach them.

Reeling Home with the Whale

After midnight church, a carol jangles my tongue.
My ten-year body, a blue spark climbing a hill.
Christmas lights across our porch flicker, rung
The snow with steps for me to follow and fill.
Never going home, I puff, not to a fragile three
Sisters dolled under quilts and no new brother.
I slide backwards across our neighbor's bluegill sea.
Its great thick skin of ice swells in the mothering
Night like a humpback whale. Half-running, flopping,
I ride his flukes beyond the edge. His flight cracks
And vooms, trills down deep from cliff to grotto.
Voices slipping on shore shout, "Come back, come back."
But me and my brother took our place in the choir
And sang to the roof of the world about the tides
Tilted off their axis, the stars harpooning our cries,
Our many unanswered prayers shot like flares in the sky.

Pruning Apple Trees on McCoy's Farm

Hardwick, Vermont

This spring,
miles out on a dirt road
centuries old with ruts and rusted plows,
I prune and pick my way through apple trees.
"Cut away enough dead limbs," Harold says,
"so we can throw a cat through."
I climb from Mackintosh to Rome to Duchess,
barefoot, happy to lean toward
the prickly May sun, hurting.
Lichen-covered bark rakes my feet
like tundra stone ten thousand years
clamped under the wind's snout.
To live here,
burrowed into elements,
with only cows, fence and clumps of granite,
you must bivouac under heaven,
twisted in drifts, sometimes brittle,
root-braced for winter,
waiting for leafy green
to strike your bud-wet surface,
all your branches listening for the first bees
itchy for a snort of pollen,
occasionally through lopped-off limbs
watching a cat sail through your forked trunk,
marking its scrambling, yowled flight
as a signal, at last,
to stand one more year
and bear on each branch the king's golden fruit.

Vermont Gray, A Train, A Boat

An all-night rain rattles my tin roof.
"Must be November," I tell my pillow.
My Vermont town puffs like a train terminal.
Each chimneyed house chugs long hours
into oncoming winter, clack, clacking
with sparks and flumes of wood smoke,
determined, by god, to be saved by next summer.

Two Novembers ago, my bones first huddled
by a Vermont blaze. There, I sifted
through our ten years together, hungering
for the blue skies we headed West for.
The past trembled like this: July night
camped below Independence Pass. Hailstones
fat as grapefruit, pelted me to the car.

You laughed, dragged me back, poor flatlander
from Florida, and zipped me up in our sleeping
bag till coffee. Like a fairweather deckhand,
I took to the bars any life knots
we couldn't untangle in a blow. I sulked,
sculled out of reach, straggled back in
from the glowing arms of a more perfect rainbow.

Vermont gray is still good for sifting ashes.
Just today, a man came to my door peddling
the end of the world. With him, I could stand
with the saved when Jehovah's fire torched
the earth. Nothing he could preach
about the paradise to follow would end our past,
would save me from the gray I sometimes come to

after I'd capsized our small boat
worked in the wood of dreams, whose planking,
edge-nailed and glued had come undone,
a craft unlike any other that we believed,
after 10 years of trials, could shoot the rapids
of one of those great flooding mountain rivers
out into the cleansing waters of the sea.

One More City on my Map

I fiddled with miniature tails
Of Louisiana crawfish, nibbled on
Brown beans and okra,
Ordered more beer and French bread
To cushion the memory
Of too many cities stacked
Like empty husks on my plate.
No, this is not Baton Rouge or Batten Kill,
But Minneapolis, home of black-eyed Chippewa,
Ol' Man River and hungry Dakota wind.
What we tell ourselves we want
From stones in the road
Never settles in until we close
The wobbly garden gate.
Then, the new city crisscrosses
In the sprawl of bridges,
Tangling Minnehaha with Hiawatha.
Rivers we choose to float us home
Change as music slides up scale
Or down the whistler's alley
Where we live alone with our questions.
This life, made for beginners
In birch-bark canoes,
Wants riddles solved,
The coiling swath of restlessness
Forgiven, all maps blessed.
I think back through canyon roads
In Wyoming, Colorado, Arizona,
To what hometown over mountains
Were they twisting me?
Of a dozen nights of love
Closing around me like the petals

Of the giant saguaro,
What invisibility did I wish to steal
From soft, scented folds?
Did I pay homage to the mysteries
That drove my paddle to this place,
Or only run ragged like the river?
This is the worst that can happen—
What Dante said Hell would grant us:
A chance to repeat our history,
Bound to the objects of desire,
Always looking to be filled up,
With more roads, more new faces,
With the flowers of the future,
Believed to outlive even flames.

For the Beluga Whales at the Minnesota Zoo

I have traveled all my life to come here,
to this viewing tank beneath ground,
where you join together
in a time-released roll,
flipping over one another's flukes,
somersaulting out of reach
and sliding the long white length back,
before you plunge
to nibble on a leaf
fallen from that changing world.
Others here stake a guarded companionship:
great horned owl and porcupine,
grey fox and raven,
and the many couples wrapped
against the first October winds,
who seldom nudge and touch each other
and trust the nature of the dance.
There, a woman with hands
cut from eternal ice.
With her, a man who has read too often
until the light turns away
and he remains an island
stranded from the great salt lane
of his children's laughter.
And who am I with my bundle
of confused voices
thrown against the door of my chest,
but another traveler
wishing for the spirit
of everlasting quiet
that sings from your skin.
Even in captivity,

far from rustling foam,
you play with the laws
of slow spiraling acceptance,
as if you never left
the ocean's night rhythms
and the miles of music between continents.

In a Rowboat on a Lake in Minnesota

Free at bow and stern, I slip away from the dock,
Rowing one oar pull at a time, taking
Each stroke through the hairs of mist
As a small, stolen promise of the lost worlds
Within me still to come, but for the shore's resistance.
Asleep next to you on a rickety cabin bed,

I was a box of joints and pulleys testing the logic
Of marriage, hoisting my hungers and questions
For approval from your face tucked between my neck
And shoulder. Here, I am something else, a movement,
As Santayana suggests of life, from the forgotten
To the unexpected, a slow moving ripple, a figure

Condensed from a greater mist to a smaller dappled
Shape not yet defined by light. How I rose to this lake
In northern Minnesota is a long winter's tale
Marked with riddles, dead-ends, kitchen arguments
With my past, our future. Whatever purity
I wanted from the storehouses of the snow,

Where we fed our first winter has now melted,
Pooled like the coming together of day and night,
A reconciliation, a caressing of colors discovered
By a man and woman who have at last forgiven
Each other their many imperfections never glimpsed
On their wedding night. Whatever I wanted is here,

If only I could hold it with my back that pulls,
With my palms that grip, with my eyes staring
Into the depths, an eye that never blinks.
"Unlocking the instant," said Buddha to the thief,

At the flickering junction of dark and light,
"Is the jewel you already possess." I remember

This story and keep rowing back up the centuries, into
This moment in May curled around a lake in the woods,
Into a passageway, a tunnel, a hole in the hedge,
Where a child slips through mist, begins to hear
The water calling out his name, telling him to listen
To the splash of slow water lapping at the oars.

Dove

Called a Jumbo Tennessee Flattop in the trade.
But the half-peeled label between her ribs
Reads—Dove, Kalamazoo, Michigan, Gibson guitar.
Found her in a Denver pawnshop, one Sunday.
No strings, no case, hung on the back wall
Between two pegs. Pawnbroker claimed Earl Scruggs,
My king, brought her in with a broken neck.
Varnish swirled, branched with hair-line cracks.
Soundhole ragged from barnstorm flatpicking.
Wood behind the pickguard scooped out, paper thin.
Her wild cherry body smudged, nicked, gouged,
Even plugged twice with mother-of-pearl.
Frets uneven, maybe warped, tuning pegs loose
And worn. Yet she gleamed amidst the heap
As any bird might, and she was cheap.
So, I strung her in my lap, blew tuning notes
Out of a harp I had brought. String by string,
I got her ready, right, and let my hands fly.
Her bass strings burst big as a kettle drum.
Her E fluttered softer than I had ever imagined.
I ran through a G scale, hit my one good run.
Old, young, this bird torn from bluegrass,
Where was she from? She knew I might fail
To play the notes I heard in my head and pitch
Her out. She knew I was only beginning to scale
Out across the far bridges, but that morning
She rose in my hands, light, springing ahead of me
In a flash, my thumb hammering the bass, on, off,
While somewhere below in the high notes
The white bird I love was born again.

Marriage in an Open Meadow

I hold this to be the highest task of a bond
between two people: that each should
stand guard over the solitude of the other.
    —Rilke

Lucky is the snake that sheds its skin
And sharpens its diamonds in the noon sun.
That simple beginning is a bonding
With the stones and sticks of the meadow.
But you come to this place, scattered
With phoebes, sparrows and the shadow
Of Mt. Kearsarge, with years of questions
Babbled at night in a very foreign tongue.
This meadow, only a temporary clearing
Among thickets and a stand of poplar,
Demands a difficult apprenticeship.
As now, in an expanding circle of friends,
No one bird song seems to reach farther
Into the future than before.
Rilke wanted only courage from his lovers.
I imagine them crouched as stone lions,
Guarding the burial chamber of a prince,
Waiting for the wind to shift over sands,
Bringing old forms back to life.
What else besides courage to let the other
Pursue the past, down the stairs,
Into the locked rooms, never polishing
Their keys, or learning the names
Of the unwished-for guests?
The great new danger is loving the distance,
The time it takes for even a warbler

To push his song across summer grass.
Like the snake, no stranger to shadow
Or sun, dream what you deserve to know.
Let your skin speak to bone
Down to the seed and stink of it.
Be with the lion, take the sleep
Of the Egyptian dead as the gust breaks
Over the tomb and nothing steps
From the darkness. Wake with the birds,
Two solitudes together against
An open sky, each invested with powers
To pilot the night's solo quest
And the morning's safe return,
Circling, always circling back
To the meadow's one hand of quiet,
For your many hands of toil
And a striving after wind.

Honeymoon at Bear Island Lake

Each honeymooned pair leaps, I suppose,
with their appropriate butterfly and crutch.
For the gypsy's Wheel of Fortune card
has always read the same in the $5 palm:
the wheel is cracked and the two halves
don't quite fit, but there is movement
creaking across the map, a deliberate flutter
that succeeds the void, and once again
the voice of the turtle lifts over the land.
As for us, we trolled for lunker walleye
near Canada, drifting through a rowboat evening
with the sleepy-scaled giants down there
in the tea-colored water suspended in ignorance
of our slice of moon. Such luxury listening
to the wind rush past the cradled lee of an island—
all thinking slowed to inevitable facts:
what ripples runs deep to the amber caverns
of the lake from which we might raise life
on gleaming hooks.
                    Beauty and Terror swirled
near at hand, twin reflections intermingled
and unfinished in us, and in the kneading gills
hung in the rock garden shimmering below.
And as we turned toward Bear Island Cove,
what flashed like a streak of minnows out of reach?
Was it the darkness that purifies all union
or the light that kills, and could this question
be answered by an ordinary fisher in this world?
Our ciphered orders had arrived from the beyond:
we would make hurried love on a raspberry bluff
before the deer flies drew blood, and later
torture wood ticks nested against the scalp,

snag no walleye from the depths, but we would shine,
embracing the wind shifts, the argumentative
oscillations, moving from decision to reproach,
from renunciation to desire, pledging to return
by oar-pull to the sources of memory and there
one jackfrost morning seek out the old fish
swinging close to the shore for a little warmth.

Part IV

To Confucius

To Confucius

What hour is this? Morning or midnight?
Could this be the time of turning when the eunuchs
no longer whisper in the emperor's ear
about the machination of the moon and stars,
when artifice crumbles, lies evaporate,
and we go back before the hurried mapmaking began,
back to the pools of memory, and begin again
to tame the williwaws gathering below the continent?
You said all the ten thousand living things
are found within us, but how are we to count
the city's scattered teeth, or explain to our children
the seed's ancient unity said to cast out
a single ripple forever?
                    Tonight, dear teacher,
sounds like no other night I can name,
as the giant tortoise scrawls no message in the sand
and the drowsy flea jumps out of the folded uniforms
and sings a little anthem to the elongated smoke.
Listen to the steps springing to the high ladders—
our watchmen climb out of their salt and oil to catch
the light glistening the bark of rain-swept pine trees,
the first stars nailing down the valley entrance.
Everywhere men kill what they claim to love.
The small pebble brain crouches like a tiger
beneath a passing cloud—all for the fruits of victory
that would turn as ashes in our mouths.

What words can we summon to break down
the old iron hills ringing between distant cities?
Where do we plant the mustard seed and purple onion,
the essence of who we are for a short while, together?

The night tethers its clock to the squeal of a swollen pig
and we shall all be changed in a moment
with our colors gone to feed the brittle spears of bamboo.
How we miss your unlikely pentangle questions now,
your refusal to begrudge the hand molding
the always too shapeless image within.

Of all the creatures snarled in the cosmos,
we must be among the poorest here, filled with noise and feathers,
and not a single nourishing oath
to drop into the confusion of the mirror.
At this hour, when the night seems to die in our arms,
what is it we need—a rock, scissors, a paper boat?
What permanence is there we can steal from shadow?
In this fix between dawn and dusk,
when the spruce and maple stand festooned
with seesawing crows, how do we enter this moment under fire,
when what wakes in heaven, sleeps again on earth?

Herman Hesse Replies to a German Actor, 1934

The oboe's thick gold resin,
An ambrosia poured along the bass of certain German songs.
Have you never heard it rising like sap from beneath
The varnished floors where you perform for the men
In uniform? As a child I ran from the smart bootstepping
Of my schoolmates, the rehearsed "yes" and "no,"
And sought my absolution in private tears
And in the dusty books of my father's shelf—
Zoroaster, Lao-tzu, Heraclitus—names
That still hold all the marrow I will ever need
From midnight. I hid behind my glasses
And my listening, and grew scared of earnest smiles
On Sunday—a day chilled by the sacrificial lamb
That marked the sum of innocence.
Did God exist to receive the gifts of the abattoir?
From the altar littered with thumping flourishes,
There was no telling when a flash
Of the ungovernable would be given a blessing.
I knew then I would one day discover
A solid walking stick for crossing the Alps
And there—in the mist-rippled ascents—
Learn to single out the cuckoo practicing its scales
Down in the valley. With the Swiss
I have stayed all these war years, and I offer
No apology for baking sugar cookies and sleeping
In the garden amid a tangle of stone lilies.
Hobbes wrote somewhere, "Evil is a robust child,"
And what part of you, smaller than the sky,
Can deny the strong-grained resolve of the fatherland?
Hatred, the old fur, bristles on cue
When the sovereign finds his child strut.
"See the enemy," he shouts, "how large

He looms on the border," but what are we
In our separate skins if not the accidents of birth
Caught between the letters of each other's
Imperishable state? I don't know how close
To your footfall the horror begins, or what needles
You must thread, but there is nothing I can do for Germany
Or for you or anyone else, nothing but dabble
In my garden, point out in simple words and stories
Where the Beast stops drawing back the windy tooth,
And something higher in us, unspoken, begins to hear
The yellow-green weaving of stems like airy strings—
Innumerable, anonymous and near at hand.

After Re-reading Moby Dick

Through candlelight flutter, creaking mast,
Smell of hawthorn and wet moss five hundred
Miles at sea, I learn again how all orders
Spin disorderly off the dog-earred charts.
The ego, that monster born of 3,000 heads,
Will bite back, swallow what flesh stands
In the hold of the sea's running luminescence,
And leave us heir to a century's twisted
Chase over the blueprint of the tides.
And to hell with joy speared from innocence.

On a night like this suspended from the hinge
Of a gull's cry, you can almost hear Ahab
Consecrating the harpoons, touch the hush
On the quarterdeck as the crew swoons
Beneath his vowels, for on this passage out
Panic will look like reason, and ordinary men
From the wharves will ride as kings in a sea
Of white belly foam, and the fat will boil from rind
Before the night stirs and swims through
The old man's only chant, "There be my whale."

One Morning Another Good Man is Gone

Where did Dick Peterson go?
Mr. Adjusted. Nice Guy. Man on Top.
He wore the executive's disguise.
No complaints, matching socks, all smiles.
Always brought daisies home.

The day of his going his face beamed
the brighter glow of a light bulb
before it pops. Help was on the way.
No more performances, today.
No more delivering bright selling images.

Some say how sharp his fear of failure
at the Great American Company, promising
so much. Or how lonely to wake up
and never once squeak out the tyrant's name
tearing at your ribs like a weed.

But what's left is a newspaper clipping:
"One morning another good man is gone."
Now you see him. Now you don't.
That's all folks. Go back to work.
A few, lonely few, can't afford to flip the page.

When they touch in themselves the same
broken man—frail, scared, impossible to reach—
who crawls out into a cornfield
with an Exacto knife, begging at long last
for swift release, forgiveness, weak is all I have,

one gift for me, alone, alone, and never comes back.

Remembering Chaney in His Silence

In your last picture,
You played a ventriloquist
Dressed as a withered biddy,
Who threw her voice three ways into shadow.
A "talkie," the papers said, but your lips
Never moved. Afterwards, you signed
Into an L.A. hospital, your larynx crippled
From years of strain, rehearsing this part
Tailored to carry you into sound.
On that bed, with cancer multiplying
Over your cords, you returned to the silence
You were born with—a little room
Where you learned the heart's flickering alphabet
From the faces your deaf-mute parents
Floated over your crib. The torn grin.
Their eyes, white and rolling, containing
Equal portions of horror and ecstasy.
That was your first art:
Loving them with their own language.
In those early shadows,
Lost to sound, you saw their hands
Claw at the undecipherable root
Of their own solitary charade.
You got lucky, broke through to the pain
Jailed in their throat,
And scalded a thousand faces
From your first tearful masquerade.
Out upon your stage,
The great sorrows took shape,
Crawled forward like the rending of metal,
Rang out even farther than the earthly end.
Such was the Phantom's stance

Cowled behind the Opera curtain.
Repulsed, charmed—
Who can say down what stairs
Your mask would lead the wavering singer?
For you her skin glowed like a scarf
Of silk tattooed with fire.
Her voice gave wings to your scars.
After years in the Paris catacombs,
Climbing, hand over hand, on a spider's thread
Into those windless places
Neighboring that angel's door,
Who can say, even now, you were wrong
To want her for your music?

With the First Snow Falling in Minneapolis: An Homage to James Wright

Lover of Appaloosa clouds and delicate bones,
You went out in the worst weather
To scout for fallen girls who held their mirrors.
Your poems became their handkerchief, their sword,
Their bread, whatever they needed to plough
Sorrow under for one more round. Outcomes
You couldn't control kept you running bitter
Into the badlands until the thin cry of horses
Sank in the sand of your chest, and you became
The flat plain between the whiskey tooth
And the train's blue whistle. Harried tales
Tracked you from Iowa to New York and beyond
To pear-tree Italy—this wanting love
To forgive you in advance, for needing it to shine
Up through the slag, but then almost dying
Before it could take you home. Your voice
Singing off-key to the broken seas of stubble,
Something about a blossom on the other side of snow.

Walking Pound's Canals

What year did he enter the labyrinth? 1908 or nine?
Something then held him: a different Venice
shaped from sand, a stone Aphrodite
risen from the Adriatic whose arms and legs
rocked him through archways, courtyards, passageways,
beneath cat-lit balconies, through filigree gardens,
alleys, overhung sidestreets, quaysides
leading him circumfluent in tongues
through every doorway, up a dizzy stairwell,
up and one day out of the chosen mosaic.

But this mud-caked city could not love him enough,
and why he hobbled from the five hundred grapevines
he planted in the castle vineyards high over Merano
is another thorn to wear down beneath the thumb.
Now, (could it be 75 years later?) the metropolis
lies betrayed. Or was it deceived, I cannot tell which.
Besieged it is and sinking into its own lagoon.
Future Atlantis whose waters lap at buildings
too old to tear down. And what the dank canals
do not erode, the clogged air will eclipse.

From this ebb, he not only mapped the universe,
he walked it from end to end, bent on the rush
of his little strut, an "idiot savant" one storekeeper
tells me, a sower of discord swept by the spirit
of gravity for a taxless federation of states,
the one American in all of Europe who could hear
the jackboot of a lost dynasty and not flinch.
I take my midday meal at the Pensione Cici
where he sat with his voices driving keel to breakers,
and listen to young neo-fascists throaty with storm.

The national speech still rings up through
a Minister of Popular Culture, up into the fugal
logic of a clairvoyant who takes to his politico
with a club. I tune out clenched fingers thumping
soup spoons and hear the Venetian encyclopedist
climbing the worm's shaggy flank with a muddy tale
all his own:
                    "The pivot of my trigonometry slipped
and the relentless ant battered at a giant's foot.
But I saw what I saw: gold strangling roots,
the forest clipped to pave an FDR troop route
through a perfect terza rima portrait: Jefferson,
Confucius and Mussolini bent over the bean rows.
Others have believed their mission rich enough
to decipher Heaven. What I wanted: an audience
equal to m'amour, for I alone could notch timber
for earth's Celestial City, dissolve the triumphs
of munition makers, money lenders, bankshark killers,
jewking usurers who never sweat a legal tender day
with their nails in dirt. God damn it, I was after

something real, something clouds could not carry
away in a pouch. Order. I SAW ORDER IN MY GARDEN.
Instead, the flowers rose like bile in the mouth.
After 13 years among cardboard walkers in the nuthouse,
silence pours through my veins, a slosh as pungent
as the mud-green tidal influx of this canal city
where I began tightening the rhythms of a century.
Possom says Dante was right. There is no direct ascent
past the beasts, and the greed for florin lives
longer than a bank loan and an old man's shallow rake."

I spoon out the question one more time:
out of all the translating, all the cross-referenced
stacks of books, what were the links with the night
to come? Who was he in his stand of dark wood?
And could the Chinese teacher he loved see his branches
as part of the tree? Back in the street
beside the Grand Canal, the churches of Guidecca
ripple in the water, porticos and cornices humbled
by a paddle's swirl, unfinished monuments
by the water's law. Transfixed or traversed?

Who can say what he felt in those last days
with so many imperfections in the text, the lacunae
glittering up before him like a galaxy,
a vast torso of scribbled notes? Unable to thread
the streets back to my hotel, I pursue Pound's
thoughts tapping cane.
                          "I will not ride the gondola,
that coffin bobbing wherever I go to catch
a sea-glimpse, that smelly crib with oars
where the chrysanthemums spill yellow and white.
I came here walking and I'll walk on from here.
Even Confucius never got the job he wanted,
so he kept to the back roads. Sirroco. Sultry.
This maze I have come to. Home to San Gregorio.
Olga waiting doorway dark. What I know
gazes before me, a lantern the dead carry.
A single sapphirine eye fixed on paradiso,
somewhere over the mountain from this tight circle
my steps will make. 'Look at Heaven there,'
my teacher would say. 'Does it speak to the tree?'"

There is a Prairie River

for Tom McGrath

There is a prairie river running up and over
A high bloodstone tabletop somewhere in North Dakota.
Slow, shallow, laden with silt,
Flowing between bluestem and needlegrass
Growing tall in tracts never cut by plow
And shaded by box elder and ash.
I think of the river there, older than barbed wire and sadness
Untying the knots in the land,
When I think of McGrath and his long American poem
That reaches down into the tenebrious agencies
Dormant in the young continent,
And returns, through famine and faithlessness,
Holding up little globes of crystal
Found in the sand of an ant hill.
See, McGrath says,
My friend the ant, the one with the tiny waist,
Has stolen the National Treasury,
And sings of future workers
Who will make and remake the world
For the joy of the great round.
It is said in an ancient Hopi tale
That to understand life
Along the vibrating centers of the earth's axis,
We must learn to shudder with faint sounds,
The body itself a tuning fork
For the unseen tintinnabulum,
The all eves ringing of unappeasable hungers
That link us to the meteoric iron and the tantivy of wild birds.
Though the Irishman from North Dakota,
Born of poor farming stock,
Is now a bit weak in the legs
And must use a cane when crossing Franklin Avenue,

He would be one of the elders chosen, as legend goes,
Who would set out over the top of the world
Wrapped in a starblanket breastplate,
Who would cast everywhere pinches of cornmeal over ashes,
And there at his feet, prairie river, rising sun.

Sunday Afternoon in the Chagall Museum

Nice, France

The barnyard ass may stagger and sway and lead us,
uprooted, into a one-cornered future,
but in Chagall's museum we are all newly married,
flying out over a golden village on a vermilion horse.
Even the sleepy-eyed French women who peddle
their rouge during the week along the promenade
and the sailors up from Toulon bored with the topless beach life,
and the silver-haired couple half-stepping
in search of a tour guide, all have turned toward
the bride and groom who ignite the darkness
with the first journey into the starfall candelabra.

Everything is remembered or forgotten. Who can say?
But here in the wedding village, whose little houses
stand low and crooked between fields and fences,
the wide-open nocturnal eye of God has come down
from the stone tablet summit, across the blackfrost
millennia, past the long governing Torah scrolls,
to watch a shawled mother milk the family cow—
always watching, the eye sees the five-fingered world
work in her, in us, in the dangling crucifix and violin,
in the fugitive Jew bound with his phylacteries
who stands up to wave hello from his careening cart.

How we ever found our way to this moment of earthly
consolation remains unwritten and untold,
but on this night of vows and kisses and long pulls
on the iced chalice of red luminous wine,
the angel blows a new moon from its trumpet
and the rooster gazes back at the eye of God,
at the sleeping village, at the man disappearing in a cart—
its arc of wobbled, high-pitched sound sending home
the last of the stray wedding party guests,
while the lovers held aloft on a sailing horse
rock and glow and ride on into the night like sabbath candles.

On Mallarmé's Plan

More lives. Who doesn't carry this hunger
Under their tongue like a good luck charm?
Why just the other night I was reading
Of Mallarmé's plan to write a book of poems
That would be a double of the cosmos,
But he never wrote the book—the pages,
Loose-leaf in his head, where you slip
Behind the backside of a mirror to watch
The faces, granite and unteachable,
Relearn the ancient calligraphy of the stars.
In the late night blur, words themselves
Will exchange places in the scribbled margin.
Potter's field, for instance, becomes *pompano*—
In just the same way the wriggling parasite
One day delivers the blistering white pearl.
The junction of the *double* is never far away.
How else can you explain the appearance of owls
Whooshing out of little woodpecker holes,
Or that my death, born with me, will leave
To inhabit some other body? There was a time
I remember on the islands north of Vancouver
When a timber wolf ran alongside me on the trail
Out of sight in the underbrush, the rapid thumping
Of his paws beating a hole inside my chest
Until there was no difference between his panting
And my trembling incantation. Moving
In unison, I became the *other*, and my body,
Lit with the darkest of the dark powers,
Drifted through the gate of the many cricket cities.
That wolf never did cross my path with a tooth,
Even so, there are nights in the forest when my belly
Is flamed by the seed of a blooming interior sun,

And no matter where I sleep, I can hear
The night's eyelid nicked by thorns, the lapping
Of waters lifted by wind, the pages turning,
The quiver of owl and pompano entangled in flight,
The book of poems completed by another hand.

Shouting to the Man in the Yang-Tse Gorge

in memory of Terrence des Pres

In this hard cool primary rain,
older than the fish,
I look for possibilities within the widest orbit
of this wobbly planet,
for some new unobstructed view,
for my breath that might carry beyond it
a portrait of the world,
for those "mists of increase"
that Strindberg hunted with a bottle of liquid lead
in the cemetery of Montparnasse.
After all, this is Spring
and once more we must decide
if the earth is a myth worth sustaining
or a piece of dirt surrounded
by ten thousand leagues of water.
I would rather believe,
so I stand here amid the elements,
thinking back to how molten lava struck bedrock,
how every single tangled strand of fire
traveled the long way toward its turning.
What blinded with rolling flame
now builds, what broke off from land mass
and drifted a mile into blackness
is now whole, an island treetop
for the toucanet and gray silky flycatcher.
The stars that once caught
our myopic amphibian stare have vanished in their tracks,
but still their glistening threads wind on,
a darkness that sends back its light
by which we make small advances.
The poets of the Yang-Tse Gorge claim
it's the rift itself that unites—

that only our defenselessness can protect against the roar.
Such puzzles as this contain both ends
of the bridge swaying above the rapids,
but I've not arrived there, yet.
What am I capable of today?
Can I stand up, shout across the gorge
without acknowledgement of being heard?
Is my voice in the rain enough
to help the man in the 8th century poem
pole across rough currents,
despite the gorge, in one place, narrow as a reed?

The Arctic Balloonists Talk
to the Ones They Left Behind

North, as always, lies the greater magnet
fixed beneath the restless ice.
No woman's shoulders are soft enough to stay home for.
No Sunday stroll compares with the soul
of a compass needle. Greatness sings
at the upper elevations, sailing beyond
familiar streets, pastry shops and churches
out where wind shakes ocean swell into ridges
and the blue-white of snow casts shadows
straight into the maw of the Pole.
We all felt this quiver and stitched glory
into a balloon launched from the top of Sweden—
A strange new *Eagle* redeeming everything
we did not accomplish with a fork, a spoon,
and a fine bottle of acquavit.
For this reason we cried nothing when ice
thickened in the shrouds, pulled us down
no matter how many times we fired the burners,
or cut ballast away from the gondola.
Only a few hours out on the wind, we beached.
The amorphous, still-swollen balloon
crept on the ice like a harpooned whale
and died. On foot, we might have straggled
south, found safety. Yet defeat stood too visible
in that direction, so we pressed north,
dragging our sleds over shifting floes.
For months, as faces blackened with frostbite,
we learned the meaning of white—the one color
into which all time dissolves
after the light of heaven turns away.
The past wrapped around us, luminous as letters
scribbled in our heads, until even the ink of memory

froze with each forward step. Broken voices
peopled the horizon. Then, they too stopped.
Whatever differences we had among us when we started
were bleached by the oncoming loneliness
of an only imagined future. And the present, my friends—
its cold alone remained for us to enter
and, of course, winter's black tent staked
in the middle of each man's dream of summer.
Towards the end, in all that whiteness going under,
something else happened more rare than apple trees:
we repeatedly brought each other back into this world
just by looking away from the gray into one another's eyes.

Playing for the Pickerel One August Night

After awakening in a blackness so thick
I was afraid I would knock against it
should I budge,
I grabbed my guitar, slipped out the window
into the muggy cornstalk Ohio night.
I climbed into my rowboat anchored in cattails,
nudged away from shore, dipped the oars
into the light-green waters
opening oceans around me.
Just the sound of splashing carried me cooler
toward the middle shine of the pond
where I began to strum my 6-string
until bluegills and pickerel lay charmed beneath me,
dozens of giants hovering in a circle
as the moon rode over the pond's ribbed bottom
and helped me pick out the melody.
Always before,
the music had dropped me lower down the neck,
somewhere deep in the unfinished song,
but that August night, I plucked
all the notes ever heard in my head.
There was no separation
between sadness and euphoria,
no obstacle between the life running over the frets,
and my future death laying down its ghost.
Alone in a rowboat,
I spun beneath the eye of the world,
an insect on a splinter,
something strong and resplendent
like a gold bug fully emerged from an apple tree knot.
Lit up with glitter,
I counted stars careening from clouds,
played all my music for the pickerel
that swayed forth from the tangled penumbral edge of the pond.

Su Tung P'O Awakens in Moonlight
to Write a Letter to His Wife

Before I left, something welled up
inside me like a moon
dragged out of the sea by a rogue wave.
As we rocked fever even into our fingertips,
fear of what the sea brings to every human coast
caved me in,
                    kept me traveling under my hat the sky
to this far-off country of gunpowder clouds
and the long chain of stars passing overhead.
But that night in the flagstone garden
the moon took on the smile
of our well-rested emperor, the older one
with no imagination for the sea's white stub.
We wrapped each other up, heard
in our nibbled leaf words
how huge a wave's crown could be
bearing down on a child's moonlit tracks.

That night, what hope did we pull
from the seaweed wreckage of his face?
How could I believe his gape would ever caress
the unborn descendants of our enemies,
serve as final proof our child would not face,
on its first day, the flash of crossed swords?
I remember all this whispering
like a man whose one quick stroke of the brush
tells the story of his whole life.
I am older now, my pennywhistle, my dear protector
of the February plum, but still I am here,
without message or instruction, learning
how to grieve for a moon hoisted by its neck
over the waters, for this letter in moonlight

cheapened by the careless gaze of kings,
for my own weakness in the crook
of this transitional season of few leaves.
Forgive me.
            There are weapons I must use
in my words I never dreamed of
when we stayed somewhere near the back roads
cradling our ordinary secrets.
Of the poet's obligation,
how could I have known its design
when I came so late to suffer the extremities
of the same god: its boot smearing
over small tracks in the breath
of a low light rising,
and this old man by a river where I wash,
who begins again the morning
by taking for a dancing partner
the crescent moon.

J. P. White was born in Akron, Ohio in 1952 and graduated from New College in 1974. The son of a sailor, he spent the summers of his childhood on Lake Erie. Since then, he has lived in Florida, Colorado, Wyoming, and Vermont. His poetry has been widely published in such journals as *The Nation*, *The Ontario Review*, *Poetry*, and *The North American Review*, and has attracted honors including an Individual Writing Fellowship from Vermont, the Minnesota State Arts Board Fellowship and the Bush Artist Fellowship. His first collection, *In Pursuit of Wings*, was published in 1978 by Panache Books. He currently lives in Minneapolis with his wife, Betty Bright, a calligrapher.

This book was typeset in Sabon by Irish Setter and printed and bound by Thomson-Shore, Inc. The cover and text were designed by John Laursen at Press-22. The cover painting is by Kathy Spalding and the calligraphy was created by Betty Bright.